Parents as Partners

Helping Your Child's

Literacy and Language

Development

First Steps was developed by the Education Department of Western Australia under the direction of Alison Dewsbury.

Rigby Heinemann

Rigby Heinemann
a division of Reed International Books Australia Pty Ltd
22 Salmon Street, Port Melbourne, Victoria 3207
World Wide Web   http://www.hi.com.au
Email   info@hi.com.au

Offices in Sydney, Brisbane, Perth and Adelaide. Associated
companies, branches and representatives throughout the world.

Published by Rigby Heinemann on behalf of the Education
Department of Western Australia

© Education Department of Western Australia
Previous edition published by Addison Wesley Longman
This edition published by Rigby Heinemann 1997

2002 2001 2000 1999
13 12 11 10 9 8 7 6 5

Cataloguing-in-Publication data

Parents as partners

National Library of Australia
ISBN 0 7312 2363 2

1. Home and school - Australia. 2. Education, Primary- Australian-
Parent participation. 1. Western Australia. Education Dept. (Series:
First Steps (Perth, W.A.)).

372.94

Contents

Schools build on the successful learning provided in the home by parents. Parents and teachers working together in partnership will help a child achieve success.

. . . at home
PARENTS:

give children support and encouragement as they 'have a go' at things. They don't expect that children will get everything right the first time around.

understand that each of their children is different and provide lots of support as they develop in different ways.

care deeply about their children, watching their progress and offering praise, help and support when it is needed.

talk things through with their children, listen to what they are saying and answer their questions.

allow their children to experiment, solve problems and try things out.

encourage children to talk about their feelings, experiences, ideas and offer suggestions.

praise children's efforts as they attempt new things. When children are encouraged to have confidence in themselves and their own abilities, the foundations for successful learning are established.

S upporting

U nderstanding

C aring

C ommunication

E xperimentation

S haring

S uccess

. . . at school
TEACHERS:

provide a supportive, accepting classroom where the needs of individuals will be met.

understand that each child is different and will need to be supported in different ways in the classroom program.

respond to the needs of all children in the class. They guide children in their efforts, offering praise, help and support when it is needed.

allow children time to interact with each other, talking through ideas, understandings and problems. They also make sure children believe and expect that they will succeed.

provide opportunities for children to experiment and solve problems in situations that make sense to them.

encourage children to discuss their ideas, how they solved problems and suggest how they could improve on their ideas.

recognise and praise children's achievements no matter how small they are. Teachers make sure all children experience success by providing a learning program that takes into account children's developing knowledge and understandings, skills and strategies.

Introduction

This book offers descriptions of the sorts of things that children are likely to do as they become increasingly literate within an English-speaking schooling system. The descriptions of children's literacy behaviours are like milestones on a map. The map enables us to track a child's literacy journey to see how far the child has travelled. It also helps us to identify the sort of assistance we can offer to provide good support for a child at each phase of the journey.

The activities, strategies and games in this book are suggested as ways in which parents can provide this support. They have been gathered largely from parents who have themselves experienced English-speaking schooling. Research recently carried out by Judith Rivalland and Caroline Barratt-Pugh of Edith Cowan University (*Breen et al. 1994) shows that parents from a range of different cultural backgrounds all support their children's learning in ways that may be very different from culture to culture, but are equally effective. A page has been included on which parents may wish to record observations and strategies of their own. It is important that parents have faith in their own knowledge and instincts so that they continue to support and help their children in the familiar ways that may already have proved to be successful.

The First Steps Consultancy Unit would be very pleased to receive ideas and suggestions from parents (especially those from the range of different cultural communities) relating to ways in which they support their children at home. These will be collated and incorporated in later editions of this book to produce a more inclusive compendium of useful strategies.

Address   First Steps Consultancy Unit
           Education Department of Western Australia
           151 Royal Street
           East Perth WA 6004

Fax   09 264 5005

Alison Dewsbury

Alison Dewsbury

* Breen J., Barratt-Pugh C., Rivalland J., and Rohl M. 1994, *Literacy in its Place, Australian Language and Literacy Policy, National Child Literacy Project Number 2*, School of Language Education, Edith Cowan University, Western Australia.

First Steps: Supporting Your Child's Language Development

Milestones of Development

People come in all sorts of shapes and sizes. They look different, sound different and behave differently. In spite of this, there is a common pattern of growth and development which can be traced from birth through to old age. Parents know and expect that their children will achieve a range of developmental milestones, such as rolling over for the first time or cutting their first teeth. Each milestone achieved is a cause for celebration and is usually lovingly remembered. Some children do everything according to 'the book'. Some take longer than others to reach milestones, some skip a few. Overall, however, the pattern of development follows a fairly predictable course.

Helping Children Reach Milestones

Most parents know instinctively how best to help their children at each phase of development. They provide a supporting hand under a new baby's head, they hang up bright mobiles to stimulate them and help them focus their gaze, and they give them things to chew on when their teeth are coming through. Later on, although growth and development continue, the changes are not quite so obvious. The difference in physical growth and development between a baby and a one year-old is very marked. The development that takes place between the ages of nine and ten may not be as noticeable but it is equally important.

Literacy Milestones

Just as the milestones of physical growth can be charted, so too can milestones of literacy development. Some children reach literacy milestones very quickly; others take longer. Some may make a few long leaps and miss a few milestones; others move steadily from one milestone to the next. Young children develop in their own good time. Just as you can't force children to grow or to walk before they can crawl, so you can't make children read, write or spell perfectly before they have reached the right sort of literacy milestones.

While children are developing at their own pace, we can give the right sort of help at the right time to help each child develop to his or her full potential. 'Maps' of language development, which we call Developmental Continua, have been drawn up to show what sorts of literacy milestones children pass as they journey towards becoming fully literate. The Continua describe the sorts of things which children can be expected to do at each phase of development.

Young Children, Reading and Writing.

First of all children learn to speak. The most important thing that young children have to learn when they are beginning to read and write is how the written language works and how it relates to speech. Later, when they are beginning to read and write, they learn that language can also be written and read. One of the most important things they need to know is how spoken language relates to written language.

Adults are so familiar with reading and writing that they do not realise how hard it can be for children to understand what is going on. There are some things that you can't *tell* children; they have to work them out gradually, using the evidence of their eyes and ears and watching what adults do. It takes children a long time to work out that:

- the flow of speech is made up of separate words. Children don't realise, for instance, that *come over here* consists of three words, because when we speak we run all our words together;
- a spoken word can be written down. At first children don't know that a specific block of print stands for a specific word;
- a written word consists of a block of print with a space on either side. If you ask young children how many words there are in the printed sentence *The cat sat on the mat.*, some might say they don't know, others might say 'Seventeen' (counting the letters) and some 'Eighteen' (counting the full stop as well).

Learning to Read and Write

The things that children think about the written language are all very logical and are based on what they have experienced. Children do not need to have lessons in discriminating letters of the alphabet because this is not a problem for them. Their challenge is to work out how language works. Through play children discover how things work, whether it is building a tower or pouring water from a jug to a mug. They need to experiment and play with language before they 'learn words' or work with sounds. It is as if language is a big jigsaw, with lots of pieces which fit together to make a whole picture. When we want to assemble a jigsaw we first have a good look at the whole picture, then we put the pieces in place by trial and error, using clues and having a go.

Helping Children to Learn

When adults start to see the world of language as children see it, they can appreciate that children need lots of experiences of all sorts over a long period of time before they get it all straight. Children need to see how all the pieces of the jigsaw fit together.

Older children need the same amount of praise and encouragement as young ones when they are learning. They need to be encouraged to try new things and they need to know what they do is valued. They will not yet be able to read and write like adults, but we can help them move from one milestone to the next to ensure that their progress is sure and steady. From early childhood through adolescence to adulthood the Developmental Continua can be used to track progress in reading, writing, spelling, speaking and listening. The Continua can also be used to help parents offer the best possible help at the right time.

Helping at Home

As parents you are probably already doing lots of things which will help your children move forward on their path to literacy. Usually when parents follow their instincts they don't go far wrong. Sometimes, however, children's learning is hindered if they are expected to do things which they are not yet 'up to'. The developmental map will be of great assistance in this area.

Putting the Pieces Together

You will notice that although reading, writing and spelling have been separated, there is a very large amount of overlap. In reality it is very difficult to divide them into separate subjects. They all develop together and have a huge effect upon each other. You can't write without reading (how may times do you re-read a letter as you are writing it?) and you certainly can't write without spelling (try!). Talking goes on all the time and underpins everything.

The different aspects of literacy have been split up only because it makes it easier to think and write about them one at a time. We always have to remember, however, that they are really all mixed up and one influences the other at all times.

Making Sense of Learning

It is very important that children are able to use their skills and apply their understandings by doing things that make sense to them (like writing a card to Nanna) rather than things which seem quite pointless (like having to learn a list of words). They need to understand the goal they are trying to reach. When children want to learn to ride a bike, they stick at it and don't mind how many times they take a tumble. They will only learn to ride by riding.

Reading and writing are just the same; the best way to learn is by reading and writing. It doesn't matter what children read and write as long as they're having a go. It doesn't matter if they make mistakes; the mistakes will help them learn. Our job is to make sure that their early experiences are fun and satisfying, so that they want to read and write in real life.

Learning is Fun

If reading and writing become boring or threatening, children won't learn effectively. Children are just like us and want to spend their time doing things they like and are successful at. It is important that we find ways of making reading satisfying and relevant — like reading comics, or the instructions for a construction kit, or the direction cards in a board game. Children can do a lot of reading outside books if they are daunted by a lot of print. The recipe for success is lots of fun, praise and a genuine interest in whatever is the current craze.

Good Luck and Good Reading!

Note

Phases are not to be equated with school year/grade levels. Also, parents shouldn't use the Developmental Continua outlines in this book (pages 8, 9, 18, 19, 28, 29, 38, 39) as prescriptive checklists, expecting their children to move through each behaviour in order. The Continua describe the sorts of things which children can be expected to do at each phase of development but individual children may exhibit a range of behaviours from various phases at any one time. Also, some children may never 'do' some behaviours. Regard the Continua outlines as an overall map of the sorts of things children do, and ask your child's teacher for further information if you need it.

Ways in which I currently help my child with:

Speaking and Listening

Reading

Writing

Spelling

What does my child particularly enjoy when:
Speaking and Listening?

Reading?

Writing?

Spelling?

What does my child find difficult when:
Speaking and Listening?

Reading?

Writing?

Spelling?

What are my child's special strengths in relation to:
Speaking and Listening?

Reading?

Writing?

Spelling?

What are my child's special interests outside school?

I would like more information about:

You may wish to share these pages with your child's teacher.

Oral Language

One of the things which makes humans different from animals is their ability to use words to communicate. Talking is one of the most important things we do in life. We get to know each other through talk. We share our thoughts and feelings through talk. We learn through talk. We teach through talk. We use talk to shape our ideas and reach into new worlds of experience.

Most children are good talkers and we should encourage this as much as we can. We sometimes feel, as parents, that very few children are good listeners, especially if we are trying to tell them something important! Children sometimes find it difficult to listen to what is actually being said; they are so busy speaking that communication can become a one-sided affair. On the other hand, children are extremely good at hearing things that are not meant for their ears!

Perhaps we need to get beyond this rather limited view of speaking and listening as separate activities and consider them together as one act of communication. We need to listen to what is being said and respond to the meaning of what we hear, gradually building up shared understanding. The best way we can help children to become effective communicators is to provide a good role model. Sometimes we are better at telling children what we want than responding to what they are saying. If we are really 'active' listeners and sensitive responders, our children will learn from us and capture the power of real communication. It is people who communicate well who make a success of their work and their lives.

In the following pages you will find the Developmental Continuum for Oral Language which you can use to follow your child's literacy development. There are also some suggestions for helping your child at each phase of development. You will already be doing many of these things, but you might find one or two new ideas that would be fun to try.

Oral Language

Phases

Phase 1: Beginning Language

In this phase children are motivated by a basic need to communicate; to understand and be understood. Language development will be influenced by the children's interactions with other language users, by the opportunities they are given to hear and use language and by their immersion in a stimulating environment.

> *Play teddy.*
> *Me jump.*
> *Tim eat.*
>
> *Daddy car.*
> *Me dress.*
> *Sue book.*

The child:

- cries, chuckles, coos, babbles, and repeats sound patterns
- constantly plays at making sounds, alone or with others
- recognises and responds to human voices
- responds to own name
- uses voice to attract attention, signify emotions e.g. anger, excitement
- voices many sounds which resemble those of mother tongue e.g. *ma-ma, da-da*
- co-ordinates gestures and words e.g. waves and says *bye*
- uses single word and two word phrases to convey meaning e.g. *drink* – I want a drink, *go way* – go away
- uses non verbal communication to support single and two-word utterances e.g. *drink* – points to the fridge
- understands more language than can be verbalised
- may make mispronunciations e.g.
tu	for cup
free	for tree
ress	for dress
rink	for drink
- mixes words e.g. *shakemilk* for milkshake
- understands simple questions
- follows simple directions e.g. *Go and get the milk*
- engages in language games e.g. *Round and round the garden, Incy Wincy Spider*

Turn to page 10 for ideas that will support your child at this phase.

Phase 2: Early Language

In this phase children's use of language becomes more refined and extended. They use language to satisfy simple social needs and to gain control of objects, people and knowledge in the environment.

> CH: *I know where my Grandma lives*
> T: *Where?*
> CH: *(points)*
> T: *When did you last see your Grandma?*
> Ch: *A long time ago.*

The child:

- experiments with sounds through rhythm and repetition
- uses own grammar style which is an approximation of adult grammar — overgeneralisations are common, e.g.
plurals	*sheeps* for sheep
verbs	*goed* for went
auxiliary verbs	*I did run fast*
pronouns	*Look at the doggie, they is big*
- begins to use endings such as *ing, ed, s*
- demonstrates an understanding of most common prepositions e.g. *on, under, front, behind*
- may make sound substitutions e.g.
b for v	*dribe* for drive
t for k	*tick* for kick
s for sh	*sip* for ship
w for r	*wabbit* for rabbit
d for th	*brudda* for brother
f for th	*free* for three
- focuses on interesting sounding words and enjoys repeating them, e.g. beautiful – *bb-oo-di-fool*
- is more aware of listener needs and begins to provide feedback information when introducing new topic e.g. *Nanna, I went shopping. Look at this.*
- refines conversational skills e.g. learns ways to enter conversation, takes turns during interaction
- engages in imaginary play, often using toys, other props or imaginary friends
- shows interest in listening to and talking about stories
- tells stories about pictures
- gives simple descriptions of past events
- begins to develop concepts about quantity, size, speed, time
- makes simple predictions about future events e.g. *We'll be going in two more sleeps*
- shows an interest in how and why
- constantly asks questions – *why, who, what, where, when*
- may demonstrate confusion between fantasy and reality e.g. *I didn't break it. Monster did.*

Turn to page 11 for ideas that will support your child at this phase.

Phase 3: Exploratory Language

In this phase children already know a great deal about language. They use language competently and include most grammatical patterns. They know that language can be used to express meaning and share experiences with others.

> Ch1: *Good morning everyone. Um, when I went to my Grandma's I saw a light brown rabbit hop into the bush.*
> T: *Where is your Grandma's house?*
> Ch1: *They're called Dowling Flats.*
> Ch2: *Our house has a flat roof.*
> Ch1: *No, not the roof. It's a building.*

The child:

- may make minor mispronunciations e.g. *s/w* for th, *fw* for sw
- has grasped most grammatical rules but may still overgeneralise e.g.
tenses	*swimmed* for swam
	keept for keep
plurals	*mouses* for mice
pronouns	*They put they book in there*
- uses more lengthy and complex sentences; sometimes overusing *and, then*
- adapts language for social control, requests and seeking information
- takes conversational turns as speaker and listener
- engages in imaginative play, using language to negotiate roles, scenes and conduct of play
- uses language to explain, enquire and compare
- makes inferences e.g. *I can't play outside if it's raining*
- describes words in terms of function e.g. *You ride a horse, You drive a car*
- projects into the future, anticipates and predicts e.g. when talking about a planned outing, *When we go to visit we'll need …*
- discusses events, concepts and objects not directly experienced e.g. life on the farm (for a city child)
- suggests possible alternatives when working out a problem e.g. *We could make a road or we could make a tower*
- uses polite conversation conventions e.g. *Excuse me*
- reflects on own and others' feelings e.g. *I got mad at Nathan when he took my toys* or *It makes you sad, does it Mum?*

Turn to page 12 for ideas that will support your child at this phase.

Phase 4: Emergent Language for Learning

In this phase children use language effectively to satisfy social and communicative needs. They also display considerable skill in responding to, and using language to satisfy, the demands of formal learning.

I'm going to tell you about yesterday when we went to the zoo. We went in the conservation room and I held a llama skin in the feeling boxes and Mrs Smith pressed the button, um, and it showed us a picture of llamas and I had a race with, um a tortoise and I won because I was faster, and . . .

The speaker/listener:

- has grasped most grammatical rules but may still overgeneralise e.g.
  verbs   *sleeped* for sleep
  plurals   *mouses* for mice
- self-corrects ungrammatical speech
- uses slang and jargon with peers
- distinguishes between language used in different situations e.g. 'home language', 'classroom' and 'playground language'
- develops specific vocabulary to suit different purposes e.g. language of description, classification, comparison, argument
- includes *when, where, who, what* when retelling an experience
- roleplays character or events encountered in stories
- demonstrates abstract thinking by using verbs e.g. *I wonder, hope, think*
- uses language to
  - describe similarities and differences
  - categorise objects, people, places, events
  - discuss cause and effect
  - reason and argue
  - predict and recall
- begins to use and understand Idioms such as *Pull up your socks!* which means 'Improve your behaviour'
- begins to understand humour in jokes and riddles
- follows more complex instructions e.g. relaying messages, home routines
- questions to clarify further information

Turn to page 13 for ideas that will support your child at this phase.

Phase 5: Consolidated Language for Learning

In this phase children use language in a variety of ways and manipulate language to suit a variety of situations. They also understand how listening, speaking, writing and reading complement each other as tools for learning.

Well, I think it was last Sunday and it was raining cats and dogs so for once my Dad let me bring my parrot, Cocka, inside, and he let her out. I just patted her neck because she doesn't fly about much, um, only when she gets mad with you. And then she started dancing with my Mum by moving up and down . . .

The speaker/listener:

- shows an increasing awareness of social conventions e.g. *Could you tell me where ...? Mrs Carrol asked if you would ...*
- reflects on own and others' feelings
- increasingly uses intonation, facial expressions and gestures as tools for communicating ideas and feelings
- communicates effectively by sharing ideas, offering advice, opinions and information
- uses jargon and slang with peers
- adds appropriate elaboration and detail to recounts and describes events, objects and concepts outside immediate experience e.g. community news
- adds evaluative comments to enhance spoken presentations
- uses similes and metaphors to enhance meaning
- continues to develop reason and logic, using more refined language
- investigates problems and sees a range of solutions
- explains cause and effect relationships
- follows more complex sequences of instructions
- listens to evaluate, draw inferences and make judgements
- initiates questions to gain clarification or further information
- negotiates with adults and peers to 'get a better deal'
- recognises that language is adapted to meet social, situational and educational needs e.g. the language of reporting is different from that of interviewing or story-telling

Turn to page 14 for ideas that will support your child at this phase.

Phase 6: Extended Language for Learning

In this phase and into their adult lives children continue to extend and refine their understandings of language. Language will be manipulated and adapted to suit a range of purposes.

. . . I generally had a good time and I'm sure everyone else did as well, but I certainly did find some things difficult at Pioneer World, particularly having to wear a hat and not being allowed to talk unless spoken to. A few things occurred there that we had a good laugh about..

The speaker/listener:

- uses appropriate language in different situations e.g. formal, informal talk
- takes into account another's point of view
- effectively monitors whether a message has been understood or not
- knows when and how to use appropriate facial expressions and gestures to communicate ideas, feelings and information
- describes events, objects and concepts outside immediate experience e.g. world news, philosophy
- draws conclusions, makes inferences and evaluates what is written and what is said
- uses appropriately specialised vocabulary in a variety of situations e.g. explanations, descriptions, debates, arguments
- selects vocabulary for impact e.g. to persuade, surprise
- uses language for independent, critical thinking
- presents a variety of arguments to support a claim
- uses oral language to make hypotheses, to plan and to influence own and others' thinking
- answers spontaneous questions in an informed, competent manner
- displays a refined and sophisticated use of language through sarcasm, jokes, subtle humour
- recognises the power of the spoken word to influence human behaviour
- refines use of language to negotiate

Turn to page 15 for ideas that will support your child at this phase.

How can I help my child with speaking and listening?

Children learn to speak well because:
- parents expect them to
- parents help them in special ways, such as simplifying their language, accepting attempts as approximations of success rather than failure and not over-correcting
- parents surround them with talk
- parents allow them to learn like children
- parents provide them with continuous examples of language which children are not expected to learn all at once
- parents value and celebrate each new step in the communication process—a new word, a learned rhyme or the first attempts at conversation.

- Surround your child with language.
- Talk to your child often, responding to and reinforcing attempts to communicate.
- Read to your child and talk about the story and pictures.
- Provide a selection of durable books with clear illustrations or photographs.
- Do things with your child that involve talking together, e.g. playing simple games, packing away toys, going shopping.
- Introduce rhymes and finger plays, e.g. *Humpty Dumpty, Twinkle, Twinkle Little Star, Round and Round the Garden Like a Teddy Bear.*
- Provide a range of toys that encourage exploration and experimentation. Promote language development by talking to and encouraging your child to form ideas and understandings about his/her world, e.g. *Let's build a tall house. It's getting higher. More blocks. Oh, no! What's happened? It's crashed!*.
- Use play equipment such as:
  - blocks
  - soft toys
  - movable toys, e.g. cars, wheels, balls, carts
  - hammering toys
  - cardboard boxes and junk materials
  - sandpit and toys
  - water trough
  - bath toys
  - musical toys.
- Talk with your child, introducing words to describe the shape, colour, movement of toys as you both play with them.

- Solve problems together, e.g. hiding and locating objects, placing shapes in a posting box.
- Read nursery rhymes, sing songs and chant chants to help your child hear the sounds and patterns of language.
- Join a playgroup.
- Enrol in a toy library.

Take every opportunity to talk with your child.

Respond to his or her attempts to communicate.

How can I help my child with speaking and listening?

Children learn to talk because they have a powerful motivation to communicate with people. They learn language not just by observing and copying, but by speaking with others as they attempt to make sense of their world.

- Listen to what your child is saying or trying to say.
- Talk to your child often.
- Provide information on 'how to talk' by valuing what your child says and providing a model of how to communicate, e.g. through initiating and maintaining conversations.
- Talk about familiar things and ensure that your child has a wide range of experiences to talk about.
- Involve your child in plans, e.g. preparing for a shopping trip or holiday.
- If your child gets stuck, help him/her to express what he/she wants to say. Your child will then understand more about language and use it effectively in many situations.
- Read a wide range of books together. Children enjoy the experience and learn to love books and reading. Books provide valuable opportunities to talk together while introducing children to the patterns and sounds of the English language.
- Continue to read 'favourite' books. Repeated readings help children make sense of print.
- Link reading, writing and talking as often as possible. For example, talk about and write a simple shopping list in front of your child. Read it together.
- Say or sing nursery rhymes and action rhymes with your child.
- Encourage your child to talk with other children. This will provide opportunities to interact with different models of language.
- Provide an example of good listening and avoid responding with 'Mmm' or 'Just a minute'.
- Talk about topics of mutual interest with the expectation that your child will listen and respond.
- Write as you or your child dictates to show relationship between written and spoken word.
  Model standard speech by repeating a phrase using an acceptable form. For example:

  Child: *I did went there.*
  Parent: *Yes, you went there.*
  Child: *All gone juice.*
  Parent: *Yes, it's all gone.*

- Provide toys and household materials that help your child learn while stimulating talk. Examples could include:
  - blocks
  - plasticine, dough or modelling clay
  - dolls and soft toys
  - movable toys, e.g. cars, balls, bikes
  - jigsaws, e.g. inset boards, posting boxes
  - cardboard boxes, cartons
  - dress-up box.
- Create an outside environment that encourages exploration and manipulation:
  - swings
  - sandpit
  - cubbyhouse.
- Play inside and outside games.
- Enrol in a toy library and book library.

Always show an interest in and value what your child says.

How can I help my child with speaking and listening?

- Observe what your child is doing and support what he/she knows.
- Listen to what your child is saying or trying to say.
- Talk about familiar things and experiences. In addition, provide a wide range of experiences and activities which will motivate your child to share ideas and understandings.
- Help with meaning, e.g. explain the meanings of words, add information to clarify understanding, or paraphrase.
- Establish a story-time routine and read a wide range of books.
- Talk about books, including print and illustrations.
- Provide books for your child to read.
- Read and teach nursery rhymes, finger plays and number rhymes.
- Tell stories such as Hans Christian Andersen's Fairytales or other traditional stories.
- Provide taped stories with read-along books. This is a worthwhile activity linking reading, talking and listening in an enjoyable way. These can be borrowed from the library.
- Provide tapes of stories and songs when travelling.
- Play games that motivate children to learn language, e.g. *I Spy*, rhyming words, finding signs along the road, jokes, riddles etc.
- Provide a dressing-up box with old clothes, shoes and hats.

Provide a variety of experiences for your child.

- Engage in activities that involve talking, writing and reading together, e.g. making a shopping list, doing the shopping, writing a letter, sending a birthday card.
- Encourage your child to tell you about what has been happening.
- Accept and praise your child's attempts to read.
- Ensure that your child sees adults reading.
- Write and display messages, e.g. 'John, collect the letters.'
- Include children in some adult conversations, so that they hear adult language use.
- Provide paper and pencils and encourage children to have-a-go at writing.
- Talk about signs, displays, advertisements etc. in the community.
- Sing alphabet songs and discuss letter names.
- Talk about your child's drawing and writing.
- Develop mathematical language and understandings through counting, sorting, matching and talking about numbers, numerals, shapes, sizes and physical properties.
- Teach your child to use the telephone.
- Join a toy library.
- Enrol in a book library.

How can I help my child with speaking and listening?

- Set aside 10-15 minutes to discuss what has happened during the day.
- Involve your child in conversations, plans and discussions.
- Ask and answer questions.
- Involve your child in adult conversations, when appropriate.
- Encourage your child to give reasons for decisions he or she has made, and use logical arguments when trying to present points of view.
- Listen carefully and clarify meaning by paraphrasing your child's contributions.
- Provide a good listening model and avoid responding with 'Mmm' or 'Just a minute'.
- Talk about topics of mutual interest with the expectation that your child will listen.
- Encourage your child to share and talk about experiences with a range of people, e.g. peers, relations, other adults.
- Teach your child to use the telephone.
- Read to your child and talk about the print and illustrations.

Encourage your child to ask questions, express ideas and opinions and share information.

- Help your child to read books brought from school, e.g. talk about the title, illustrations and content.
- Ask your child to retell a story or explain a favourite section.
- Point out similarities in the way words look or sound.
- Read school newsletters together.
- Take an interest in writing produced at school.
- Talk about the purposes for writing, e.g. to make a shopping list, send a birthday card, write a letter. Show different ways of writing and provide paper and pencils for your child to have-a-go.
- Talk about the variety of print forms in magazines, newspapers, telephone books, comics.
- Focus on the message children assign to their writing rather than correct letter formations or spelling.
- Play language games, e.g. *I Spy*, rhyming words, locating signs along the road, telling jokes and riddles.
- Play games such as *Scrabble*, *Chinese Checkers*, *Snakes and Ladders*.
- Watch and discuss television programs or videos.
- Make sure that mealtimes are talking times. Encourage all family members to participate.
- Join a book library and toy library.

How can I help my child with speaking and listening?

- Set aside 10-15 minutes to discuss what has happened during the day.
- Involve your child in conversations, plans and discussions.
- Ask and answer questions.
- Encourage your child to express and justify opinions, develop logical arguments, and give reasons for decisions made.
- Involve your child in adult conversations, when appropriate. These experiences will help develop an awareness of how they and others use language.
- Provide a good listening model by showing interest in, and responding to, your child's contributions. For example, use mealtimes for discussion and encourage all family members to participate.
- Talk about topics of mutual interest and expect that your child will listen and respond.
- Provide a wide variety of books such as traditional stories, magazines, comics, atlases, dictionaries and reference books.
- Read serials or short stories.
- Encourage your child to read for pleasure.
- Compare similarities and differences between a book your child has read and its movie version, e.g. *The Secret Garden, Chitty Chitty Bang Bang* or *Winnie The Pooh*.
- Talk about current affairs viewed on television. If possible, find and read the corresponding newspaper reports.
- If your child shows an interest in a television or sports personality, make a note of any photographs or newspaper reports. Read and discuss the information with your child.
- Talk about special events or family celebrations. Encourage your child to create cards, invitations or greetings.
- Encourage your child to practise a variety of writing forms such as letters, lists and messages.
- When your child asks how to spell a word, encourage a 'have-a-go first' approach.
- Play language games such as 'I Spy' and 'Hang the Man'.
- Play commercial games which focus on word building or word knowledge.
- Include the family in games which provide enjoyment and teach social skills, e.g. taking turns, explaining rules to another player, congratulating the winner.

- Encourage your child to entertain the family with simple plays, puppet shows or jokes.
- Ask your child to recount and evaluate experiences, e.g. weekly Tee-ball or football matches.
- Involve your child in planning for holidays. Provide such items such as road maps, travel brochures, a calendar, and paper and pencils for making lists, writing reminders etc.
- Show your child how to locate a street or suburb using a street directory.
- Teach your child how to use a telephone, and locate names in a directory.
- Use your local library.

Involve your child in conversations, plans and discussions in a variety of situations.

How can I help my child with speaking and listening?

- Encourage your child to develop a positive attitude towards speaking and listening so he/she will continue to develop confidence and a willingness to share ideas, feelings and experiences.
- Discuss school work, successes, concerns, interests and personal experiences.
- Respect your child's ideas, opinions and feelings. Encourage discussion which motivates your child to elaborate ideas, justify opinions, develop logical arguments and express feelings.
- Involve your child in adult conversations, when appropriate. These experiences will provide a range of language styles, ideas and vocabulary.
- Assist your child to express ideas in an orderly, fluent manner. For example, ask for an explanation of a game, a description of an item or a recount of an experience.
- Help your child to extend the range of words understood and used by introducing specialised vocabulary when talking about topics of mutual interest, e.g. current affairs or computer programs.
- Encourage your child to listen and respond courteously and appropriately to others, even when opinions expressed may differ from his or her own.
- Provide opportunities for your child to speak and listen for a variety of purposes, e.g. telling jokes and riddles for enjoyment, explaining or giving directions, describing and elaborating on details, predicting and justifying, or identifying cause and effect.
- Provide a good listening model by showing interest in, and responding to, your child's contributions. For example, discuss issues at mealtimes and encourage all family members to participate.
- Provide a wide range of reading materials and encourage your child to read and share ideas and opinions.
- Talk about school topics and assignments. Assist your child to locate and organise information from reference books, encyclopaedias etc. Talk about layout, contents, index, glossary etc.
- Assist your child to locate information in the community, e.g. the local library, city council, community service groups.
- Compare similarities and differences between a book your child has read and its movie version.
- Watch and discuss television news reports and current affairs programs. If a particular interest is shown in a subject or event, encourage your child to look for follow-up information in newspapers.

- Discuss the effects of language on the behaviour of others, e.g. the effects of advertising or the methods used to persuade people to watch or listen to certain television or radio programs.
- Buy puzzle books that include word games.
- Play commercial games that have a focus on word building and word knowledge.
- Talk about ways to remember how to spell difficult words, e.g. 'practice' the noun, has the noun 'ice' within it.
- Talk about the relationships between words, e.g. unicycle, bicycle and tricycle and linked by the word 'cycle'.
- Show your child how to use informational books found in your home, e.g. phone and street directories, encyclopaedias, dictionaries, atlases.
- Use your local library.

Encourage your child to listen and respond to others' opinions. Support your child in developing confidence to express his or her understanding and thoughts.

Reading

People read for all sorts of reasons — for pleasure, to find out things, to follow directions, to keep in touch with friends and so on. The purpose of reading is to make sense of what we read, whether it be a book, a recipe, a road sign or a prescription.

We all interpret what we are reading in different ways, according to our ideas, experiences and the way we feel. Reading a book is rather like meeting a person; we all get slightly different impressions and would describe the person in a variety of different ways. Books mean different things to different people. We need to encourage children to make connections between what they are reading and their own experience, knowledge and ideas. Talk about books and what they mean to you. It is important that reading is seen to be an activity which is highly valued at home.

When children are young, they love to listen to stories. They focus entirely on the meaning of a book and use books as passports into magic worlds. When they go to school it sometimes seems that their reading turns into a struggle to read words and they may lose their focus on meaning. We must always help them to see that it is the meaning that matters, words are just a means to an end. If children are thinking about meaning they can guess a word or two here and there and not lose meaning. Good readers often do this.

Children don't need to read 'good' books all the time. Sometimes they like comics, joke books or computer manuals. It doesn't matter what they read as long as they are reading and enjoying it. Our most important task as parents is to give our children the opportunity to get hold of all the books they want and to let them see you enjoying reading. Thank goodness libraries are such wonderful places!

In the following pages you will find the Developmental Continuum for Reading which you can use to follow your child's literacy development. There are also some suggestions for helping your child at each phase of development. You will already be doing many of these things, but you might find one or two new ideas that would be fun to try.

Reading

Phases

Phase 1: Role Play Reading

In this phase readers show an interest in books and the print they see around them. They imitate the things they see adult readers doing such as holding the book carefully, turning the pages and talking out loud as they do so. They often retell stories they have heard as they pretend to read.

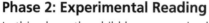

The child:
- imitates 'adult' reading behaviours
  - holds the book the right way up
  - turns the pages
  - looks at words and pictures
  - talks about the pictures, sometimes making up or retelling stories as the pages are turned
- realises that print carries a message but may read the writing differently every time e.g. when 'reading' a scribble message to parents
- knows that writing and drawing are different, for example, *Mummy reads the black bits*
- recognises own name or part of it in print
- is beginning to recognise and name some letters
- reacts to environmental print, for example, noticing the fast food sign, says *I want a hamburger*
- selects favourite books, for example, selects a book and says *I want 'The Three Little Pigs'*
- is curious about print e.g. *What does this say?*
- enjoys stories and asks for them to be read and re-read
- talks about own experience relating it to the story being read e.g. *That looks like my dog*
- will often be prompted by a picture to talk about a story that is related

Turn to page 20 for ideas that will support your child at this phase.

Phase 2: Experimental Reading

In this phase the child has memorised familiar stories and can match some spoken and written words. The reader realises that the words of print always stay the same and begins pointing to words.

The child:
- is beginning to match some spoken words with written words
- realises that the words of print always stay the same and will tell adults if they miss a word or page out when reading
- recognises some familiar words and letters, especially letters from own name and print they see around them
- is beginning to use words relating to books such as *letter, cover, page*
- has an increasing knowledge of letter names and the links between the letters and the sounds they represent
- uses background knowledge and pictures as an aid to meaning
- attempts to identify some words using the initial letter
- recognises distinctive words that catch the imagination, e.g. *engine, helicopter, dinosaur*
- focuses entirely on meaning and is not concerned with accuracy
- sees self as a reader and talks about own reading
- knows that the reading of text goes from left to right and generally top to bottom of page

Turn to page 21 for ideas that will support your child at this phase.

Phase 3: Early Reading

In this phase children may read slowly and deliberately as they try to read exactly what is on the page, rather than concentrate on the meaning. They are beginning to realise that it is good to comment on books they have read or listened to.

The child:
- can read some common words in a variety of situations, e.g. in a book, on a sign, on a card
- retells events in a story with a high degree of accuracy and detail. Talks about characters, settings and events, comparing them with own experiences
- may read word-by-word when reading unfamiliar books. Fluency and expression become stilted as the child focuses on sounding out words
- relies heavily on the beginning letters when sounding out words
- relies on sounding out for word identification and may lose the important strategies of taking risks and having a go
- sometimes guesses words that make sense when reading and reads on effectively when not interrupted
- if prompted, will re-read in order to clarify meaning that has been lost due to word-by-word reading
- is beginning to correct own reading spontaneously, but loses confidence to do this if constantly corrected by adult
- points as an aid to reading
- talks about texts being written by authors
- can identify and talk about different forms of texts e.g. recipes, lists, letters, newspaper articles
- reads familiar texts confidently but may lose fluency when reading unfamiliar texts

Turn to page 22 for ideas that will support your child at this phase.

Phase 4: Transitional Reading

In this phase readers are moving beyond a heavy reliance on sounding out as a way of working out unfamiliar words. They are able to use methods such as substituting a word that makes sense; reading on to discover the meaning; slowing down; or using their background knowledge. They are able to change their reading style to meet the demands of different types of text e.g. looking for information by skimming, or scanning the headings and sub-headings.

The reader:

- recognises an increasing number of common words
- uses a range of different methods to obtain meaning e.g. reads on when encountering a difficult text, uses pictures, illustrations and blurb; uses glossary
- self corrects when reading
- has a go at unfamiliar words
- re-reads to clarify meaning
- slows down when reading difficult text
- reads aloud when reading difficult text
- uses background knowledge to help understand what is read
- uses knowledge of different print layouts to help understanding e.g. looks for headings in a text book, uses index to locate particular information
- may read a word incorrectly, but the substitution makes sense because it fits in the sentence grammatically and captures the meaning of the original e.g. 'cool' drink for 'cold' drink
- pays attention to punctuation when reading aloud
- reads fluently and with expression when reading rehearsed material for an audience
- reads for a range of purposes e.g. for information and for pleasure
- has favourite authors and preferences for certain types of books
- sounds out or syllabifies words to help work out an unfamiliar word
- discusses how characters can be stereotyped in text and how real life is different e.g. mother looking after children and father going out to work
- talks about own interpretations of texts e.g. explains why they felt that the treatment of convicts was unfair

Turn to page 23 for ideas that will support your child at this phase.

Phase 5: Independent Reading

In this phase the reader understands and uses a wide range of techniques to comprehend different types of texts. Reading is automatic. When the reader encounters difficult texts, he or she is able to make decisions about how to deal with the material.

The reader:

- reads and comprehends material that is abstract and removed from personal experience
- makes inferences using information that is implicit, but not stated, in the text
- is able to appreciate several points of view and alternative interpretations of text
- is able to provide evidence to support own interpretations
- uses a range of techniques automatically when reading e.g. self corrects, re-reads, reads on, slows down, sub-vocalises
- is able to infer the meaning of unknown words from the context
- comments and makes judgements on the way authors represent people from different cultural and socio-economic groups
- discusses issues and topics that have emerged when reading, commenting critically on news items, magazine articles, advertisements and letters in the press
- may disagree with other people's interpretations of a text and can justify own interpretation
- sees books as a major source of information
- feels strongly about reading preferences and can justify opinions
- is totally absorbed when reading
- compares texts critically
- can relate different parts of text
- can identify the different text forms and the parts of them e.g. reports, procedures, biographies

Turn to page 24 for ideas that will support your child at this phase.

How can I help my child with reading?

- Read to your child as often as you can.
- Encourage your child to choose the books you read together and help the child to tell the story from pictures in the book.
- Talk about the books you read and the people, things and animals in them.
- Draw attention to the illustrations when reading to your child.
- Enrol your child in the local library.
- Select books that describe familiar experiences, concepts and objects as well as fairy tales and fantasy stories.
- Make sure your child sees members of the family reading.
- Buy books as presents. Let your child help you choose them.
- Keep audio tapes of favourite stories and songs in the car to play on long journeys.
- Help your child to recognise his/her own name. Write simple dedications inside the child's own books and encourage them to start building their own book collection.
- Teach your child nursery rhymes and songs.
- Make use of quality 'book and tape' sets during busy times in the daily schedule.
- Select books that use repetition to capture the rhythm of language, e.g. *The Three Billy Goats Gruff*.
- Tell stories on the way to the shop, at bath time, at bed time.
- Always keep a selection of books in your bag.
- Place labels around the home, e.g. 'These are Kim's favourite books.'
- Hold the book so the child can see the pictures and writing.
- Let the child hold the book and turn the pages.
- Encourage the child to join in and 'read' too.
- Leave the book handy for private readings to teddy.
- Help your child to tell the story from the pictures in the book.
- Talk about everyday print, e.g. "We are going in here to get a hamburger. See the sign. It says 'Harry's Hamburgers'."
- Sometimes point to the words as you read.

- Talk about your plans, e.g. 'Today I am going to make a cake, let's look at the recipe.'
- Before beginning to read, settle your child down and talk a little about the book, e.g. 'This looks as if it's going to be a funny story.'
- Accept and praise your child's attempts to read.
- Visit the local book shop.
- Fill your child's room with posters, books, pictures, mobiles of book characters.
- Make a cloth book bag to take books with you wherever you go.

Read to your child every day.

How can I help my child with reading?

- Read to your child whenever you can. Now and again ask a few 'why' questions about the story as you read.
- Help your child to tell stories from pictures in the book.
- Talk about the characters, plots and settings of stories.
- Discuss information gleaned from factual books.
- Enrol your child in the local library. Choose books together.
- Talk about reading the newspaper, magazines and books.
- Encourage your child to try and write his/her own name in books he/she owns.
- Read books of children's poetry with your child.
- Borrow 'book and tape' sets from the library.
- Compare events and people in books with your own lives.
- Talk about the pictures when reading to your child.
- Tell stories and sing songs in the car, at bath time, at bed time.
- Take books with you when visiting.
- Draw attention to print on packages, jars, e.g. 'Here is the Readybrek. This says, *Readybrek*.' Point to print.
- Let your child 'read' to you and to anyone who is willing to listen e.g. grandparents, neighbours, even the cat!
- Encourage the child to join in when reading familiar stories.

- Talk about everyday print. Discuss advertisements and talk about the effect they have on you.
- Point out interesting or long words in books.
- Accept your child's efforts without criticism. Always encourage and praise his or her efforts.
- Print your child's name while the child watches when labelling lunch box etc.
- Read birthday cards with your child, pointing to the words.
- Write shopping lists in front of your child and talk about what you are doing.
- Set up a home message board and write a message everyday, e.g. 'Today we are going to grandma's.'
- Leave plenty of scrap paper, pencils and crayons on the child's table or desk. Give him/her old diaries or inexpensive notebooks.
- Encourage your child to write messages for different family members.
- Encourage your child to find words that begin with the same letter as his/her name.
- Recognise letters on car numberplates.
- Watch and talk about television with your child.
- Encourage your child to look at the title and cover of a book and guess what it may be about.
- Encourage your child to tell the story from the pictures in the book.

Encourage your child to join in and read too.

How can I help my child with reading?

- Continue to read to your child every day. Vary the type of books read, e.g. short stories, poems or serialise long stories.
- Emphasise with your child the importance of making sense from their reading. Encourage them to take risks and 'have a go' at a word.
- De-emphasise the need to get 100% accuracy and try strategies other than sounding out.
- When reading to your child stop sometimes and ask 'What do you think might happen next?' Accept the child's answers even though they may not seem right.
- Occasionally ask some 'why' questions about the story, e.g. 'Why do you think the author put that bit in the story?'
- Talk about books your child has read at school.
- Take your child to the local library regularly and to any story telling sessions that are advertised.
- Buy books as presents to commemorate special occasions.
- Talk about the things you read — newspapers, magazines, books etc.
- Browse together in bookshops.
- Discuss and point out how to locate particular books in bookshops e.g. travel books, cooking books, computer texts.
- Talk about books you are reading together. Compare characters with real people.
- Accept your child's efforts with praise, concentrate on all the things he/she does right, not on the few errors.
- Have plenty of scrap paper, pencils, felt pens and crayons on the child's table or desk. Give a diary, birthday book or notebook for Christmas.
- Talk about illustrations to see if they match what is in the child's or your mind.
- Leave notes around the house or under your child's pillow.
- Point out the author's name before reading a book and encourage your child to read other books by that author.
- If your child makes a mistake when he or she is reading aloud, allow time for self-correction. If the mistake makes sense, ignore it.
- Encourage your child to write messages to other family members.
- Encourage your child to write letters, postcards, lists, messages. Accept spelling mistakes.

- Encourage your child to make birthday, Christmas and Easter cards, party invitations. Children can write their own greetings and verses.
- Buy your child games that provide simple instructions to read and follow. Play word games.
- Look at the TV guide together and choose a program to watch.
- Encourage your child to make up plays for the family, acting out stories. Some children like to write simple scripts and to draw up a plan for other children to follow.
- Share letters and postcards from friends with the whole family.
- Encourage your child to keep a diary or journal when you go on holidays. This is particularly valuable if you are travelling and your child is missing school.
- Play numberplate games in the car, e.g. 'silly sentences'—FCF could be 'Fat Cows Flying'.
- Encourage children to retell stories. Involve the family in swapping stories, e.g. 'I'll tell you a story if you tell me one.'

Ensure that all reading experiences are enjoyable.

How can I help my child with reading?

- Continue to read to your child if he/she enjoys it.
- Include humorous books when selecting books to read. Encourage your child to make up jokes or riddles, or humorous stories.
- Encourage your child to go to the local library regularly.
- Make sure you read some of the books your child enjoys so that you can share reactions and pleasure together.
- Ensure that your child knows what you value and enjoy reading yourself.
- Give your child book plates to stick inside his/her books.
- Encourage your child to draw and write about books and to write stories or factual information for others to read.
- Encourage your child to read to younger brothers and sisters.
- Read books that have been made into films or videos and encourage your child to talk about the differences between the books and the video or film.
- Ask your child what word would make sense when he/she becomes 'stuck' on a word. Encourage your child to have-a-go and read on to get the overall meaning.
- Select a simple child's cookery book from the library and plan a cooking session. Encourage your child to read and follow the instructions.
- Encourage your child to find an interesting article/photograph from a newspaper and tell you about it. Suggest that it be taken to school and read/discussed with the class.
- Discuss favourite authors together and decide why you like them.
- If a child makes a mistake when reading aloud, don't interrupt the reading, allow time for self-correction. If the mistake doesn't alter the meaning, let it go.
- Draw the child's attention to weather patterns displayed in the paper and relate these to televised weather reports.
- Encourage your child to read and write letters, postcards, lists and messages. Accept spelling inventions. Provide attractive paper and unusual pens.
- Encourage your child to make birthday, Christmas and Easter party invitations. The child can write his/her own greetings and verses. You may even be able to make recycled paper together.

- Buy your child games that provide simple instructions to be read and followed. Play word games together.
- Encourage your child to enter competitions in the local newspapers or magazines.
- Encourage your child to make up, and perform, plays for the family, using own and other stories. Some children like to write simple scripts or draw up a plan for other children to follow.
- Continue to play numberplate games in the car. Relate numbers to letters of the alphabet, e.g. 372=cgb=Can't Go Back.
- Encourage your child to keep a diary or journal when on holiday. This is particularly valuable if you are travelling and the child is missing school.
- Involve your child in planning for holidays. Ask the child to list all the things to be taken. Obtain a map of the area and discuss the route you will be taking. Point out signs along the way.
- Encourage your child to help you find a particular street when you are using a street directory.
- Encourage your child to retell stories. Involve the family in swapping stories, e.g. 'I'll tell you a story if you tell me one.'
- Assist your child with meaning and interpretation by paraphrasing. This is useful for school projects and assignments.

Encourage children to select their own books to read.

How can I help my child with reading?

- Recognise and be proud of your child's successes in reading.
- Ensure your child is exposed to a wide range of reading materials, i.e. newspapers, letters, recipes, TV guides, magazines, puzzle books.
- Provide a quiet, well-lit study area.
- Help your child with a time plan for homework.
- Assist with goal setting.
- Make sure your child uses the library regularly and encourage him/her to take younger children along.
- Encourage your child to read for different purposes, i.e.
  - reading biographies and novels
  - reading and explaining instructions for using new appliances
  - reading interesting articles from the community newspaper
  - reading to younger brother and sister
  - reading to find out more information about a topic.
- Take an interest in books written by favourite authors. Talk about them. Give them for presents.
- Encourage your child to talk about books he or she has enjoyed or disliked. Foster thoughtful criticism and comment.
- Support the learning process by guiding and advising. This doesn't mean doing the work for your child. Talking things through is very important.
- Talk to your child's teacher about homework expectations. Ask if there is anything further you can do to help.

- Let your child see that you sometimes need to discuss and clarify issues to help your understanding.
- Support your child's school research tasks by:
  - taking your child to the local library to find appropriate books
  - encouraging your child to jot down key issues about a topic
  - helping your child to classify this information
  - encouraging your child to explore the topic further by brainstorming topic-related questions using a 'Question Word' framework—'Who', 'How', 'When', 'If', 'Where', 'What', 'Why'.
  - encouraging your child to use the following procedures when taking notes, e.g.

    Short Notes
    key words and phrases with the
    reference book open
    Long Notes
    own sentences with
    the reference book closed.

- continue to discuss ideas, statements and underlying beliefs which are evident in newspapers, books and television programs.

Recognise your child's successes in reading and offer praise.

How we can help each other with reading?

- Look for opportunities to discuss and share excerpts and ideas from a variety of different reading materials.
- Value your own reading and be informed by that of your child. Widen each other's horizons.
- Discuss ways in which tasks can be handled. Recall strategies that have been effective in the past.
- Recognise that both you and your child may have quite different ideas about what you want to read and respect choices made. Broaden reading experiences by exchanging books.
- Provide a quiet, well-lit study area.
- Provide a range of reading matter.
- Swap magazines.
- Use second-hand book shops.

Value your own reading and share your reading experiences with others.

Writing

When we write, we have to attend to a great many things at the same time. First we need to consider who the writing is for and what sort of form it will take, for instance, a letter to a friend, a shopping list for myself or an invoice for a customer.

After deciding what we are going to write, we need to think what we want to say. Then we choose the words that best suit our purpose and make decisions about spelling, punctuation, and how to get our message across. Unless we are writing for ourselves, we try to write legibly.

As we write we are constantly reading and re-reading what we have written, making alterations and corrections as we go. At the end we look through our writing again to make sure we haven't missed a spelling error and to check that the writing reads well.

Children find writing a great challenge. They need a lot of encouragement and praise as they move through their school years. When they show you their work, pay careful attention to *what* they are writing, because that is the most important thing. Writing is like a jigsaw. It is made up of lots of little bits, but it is the big picture that counts.

Try to focus on all the good things children do, rather than on their mistakes. Sometimes children will seem to go backwards. This usually means they are coming to grips with something new, and can't deal with everything else as well. Be patient and they will soon get it all together again. The key is to make sure they remain confident and enjoy writing — the rest will follow as they gradually mature!

In the following pages you will find the Developmental Continuum for writing which you can use to follow your child's literacy development. There are also some suggestions for helping your child at each phase of development. You will already be doing many of these things, but you might find one or two new ideas that would be fun to try.

Writing

Phases

Phase 1: Role Play Writing

In this phase children are experimenting with marks on paper to try and work out the connection between the spoken and written language. They scribble and make marks on paper as they copy adult writing and sometimes try to communicate a message through their scribble.

Phase 2: Experimental Writing

In this phase children know that speech can be written down and that print remains constant. They understand that writing goes from left to right and they experiment with writing letters and words.

Phase 3: Early Writing

In this phase children write about things that are personally significant to them. They are beginning to write for people other than their teacher or parent. They know what they want to write and struggle to put it on paper. If they are concentrating on one thing they often lose control over another, for example, if they concentrate on neat printing or on spelling they may 'lose' what they want to say.

The writer:
- makes random marks on paper
- produces circular scribble with no obvious 'writing' intention
- scribbles in lines, sometimes with breaks in the scribble. If the child is right-handed the scribble often goes from left to right
- draws symbols consisting of straight and curved lines that look like letters
- mixes letters, numbers and invented letters together
- experiments with letter shapes, often reversing them or producing mirror images
- copies the form of some types of writing such as letters and lists. Fills in forms such as bank slips with neat scribble
- mixes up capital and small letters, usually preferring to use capital letters
- copies print they see around them such as the name of the fridge
- shows beginning awareness that writing goes from left to right and from top to bottom on a page
- role-plays writing messages for a purpose e.g. telephone messages, shopping lists
- recognises own name in print and attempts to write it
- often repeatedly uses first letter and other letters from name or other well-known source when writing. Eloise, for example, will use E, S, L with other letter-like marks
- sometimes thinks that own writing can be read by others
- understands that writing and drawing are different, but may mix them up

Turn to page 30 for ideas that will support your child at this phase.

The writer:
- tries to read back own writing
- knows that the written message stays the same, but does not always 'read' it the same way
- voices thoughts while writing
- mixes up capitals and small letters
- can tell the difference between numbers and letters
- 'writes' from left to right and top to bottom on a page
- starts to leave spaces between 'words'
- shows that one letter or letter cluster represents one word
- repeats familiar words when writing, e.g. *I like cats. I like dogs*, but will probably not write these words in conventional ways
- starts to notice features like full stops and commas and 'sprinkle' them through their writing
- dictates slowly when adult is writing for them
- writes different forms that are familiar e.g. letters, lists, telephone messages, stories, greeting cards

Turn to page 31 for ideas that will support your child at this phase.

The writer:
- uses a small range of familiar forms of writing e.g. letters, stories, recipes, lists
- often writes about personal events e.g. holidays, pets or something that has happened
- writes in sentences that may or may not have correct punctuation
- uses words such as 'and then' rather a lot
- uses words which have personal significance and may be part of a current craze, from television, books, playground play
- may begin to make simple corrections. May be overwhelmed if asked to correct writing of which they are very proud
- attempts to use some punctuation such as full stops, capital letters, question marks
- starts to use the language they have heard from books, films or television such as *Once in a galaxy, far, far away...*
- sometimes writes on the same topic or uses the same sentence beginnings again and again, as confidence is built and control is gained over the different elements of writing
- talks with others to plan and revise own writing
- re-reads writing to check if it makes sense
- provides some detail and description in writing
- is keen to complete their writing

Turn to page 32 for ideas that will support your child at this phase.

Phase 4: Conventional Writing

In this phase writers know most of the basic elements of the writing process. They are able to choose different types of writing to suit different purposes. When they are focusing on learning a new skill they often appear to regress in other areas.

Phase 5: Proficient Writing

In this phase writers have developed a personal style of writing and can adapt different forms of text to suit different purposes and audiences. They have control over spelling and punctuation and select appropriate words from a wide vocabulary. Proficient writing skills will probably develop in secondary school. Primary school children are not expected to be working in this phase.

The First Boomerang

One day, many years ago, there lived an aboriginal carpenter named Kesaw. He was well respected by his tribe and was noted for his creative sculptures. For many years he had carved creatures from the local jarrah trees.
As he sat in the warm spring sun a sleepy snake slithered by. Kesaw decided to carve a snake. Slowly he got up to find the right piece of wood. When he was satisfied with his selection he began to whittle away with his best blade. The wood was hard and the carving slow. Kesaw began to get drowsy. His head nodded and he fell asleep.

Our Heritage

Many of the people who want to save the trees talk of history and heritage. The tree was a meeting place, a place of happiness, a source of shade on burning summer days after a refreshing swim in the nearby river. But then the traffic built up, the river became a murky passage of sludge. The children grew up and had their own children, but their children knew nothing of this once peaceful place.

The writer

- uses different forms of writing to suit different purposes e.g. an explanation in social studies, an experiment in science, a procedure in mathematics
- uses knowledge of other texts as models for writing
- plans before starting to write
- considers the needs of the reader and includes essential background information
- starts to use headings and sub-headings to organise the writing
- can use information from reading in writing e.g. takes notes from an encyclopaedia for a project
- groups sentences which contain related information into paragraphs
- links ideas together to form a logical piece of writing
- sentences vary in length, organisation and complexity
- selects vocabulary appropriate to specific curriculum areas
- proof reads and edits own work reasonably well
- enjoys having fun with language e.g. puns on names such as 'Pittsville'
- begins to adjust vocabulary according to audience e.g. when writing a story for young children will include less complex vocabulary than would use in a story for adults

Turn to page 34 for ideas that will support your child at this phase.

The writer

- demonstrates success in writing a wide range of different types of writing
- sustains coherence and cohesion throughout writing
- demonstrates ability to view writing from a reader's perspective
- consciously varies writing to suit audience needs
- uses a wide range of words that clearly and precisely convey meaning in a particular piece of writing
- uses a variety of simple, compound and complex sentences appropriate to text form
- edits own writing independently, during and after composing
- selects and makes appropriate use of writing conventions e.g. punctuation, grammar, organisation, presentation and layout
- is beginning to convey mood, atmosphere and shades of meaning
- takes notes, selects and synthesises relevant information and uses plans when writing

Turn to page 35 for ideas that will support your child at this phase.

29

How can I help my child with writing?

- Find time to show your child that you value reading and writing for yourself, and share reading and writing with them. Reading teaches children many things about writing and experimenting with writing helps children develop their understandings about reading.
- Take your child to the library and encourage them to select their own books.
- Share simple picture storybooks whenever you can. Talk about the pictures and story and relate events or characters to your child's experiences. Encourage questions and predictions about the stories.
- Read and sing nursery rhymes with your child. Use as many action rhymes as possible, such as 'one little piggy went to market' or 'pattacake…'
- Read books which feature rhyme and repetition. Sometimes point to the words as they are read. Encourage your child to join in and to predict which words come next.
- Talk about the events of the day encouraging your child to join in.
- Talk about print in the environment, e.g. stop signs, advertisements.
- Show your child how you use writing. Write messages, shopping lists, telephone messages, letters and greeting cards in front of him/her and talk about what you are doing.
- Provide a special place for your child to write. Equipment such as a small table or desk, an easel-type blackboard and a notice board for displaying writing plus a range of writing materials such as scrap paper (lined, coloured or plain), used greeting cards, crayons, bank forms, mail order forms, envelopes and little note-books would provide an excellent environment for children to experiment with writing.
- Find opportunities to display your child's name.
- When your child asks about letters of the alphabet, call the letters by their names not the sounds they may represent.
- Talk about alphabet books and answer children's questions.
- Provide magnetic or plastic letter tiles for children's play.
- Allow your child to use a typewriter or word processor to play with and write messages. He or she may discover some letters from his or her name.
- Write messages for your child to read, e.g. Please feed the cat, Kim. Please phone Nanna.
- Play rhyming games like 'I spy…'

- Respond positively to the message in your children's 'writing' rather than the letter formations or spelling. Celebrate children's efforts and encourage them to have-a-go at writing.

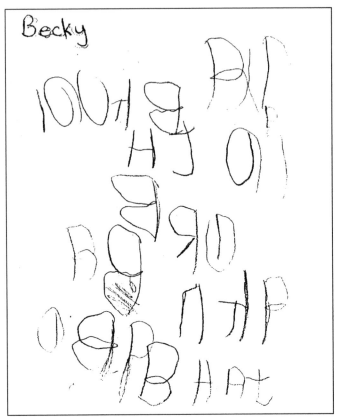

Becky: 'I made my shopping list.'

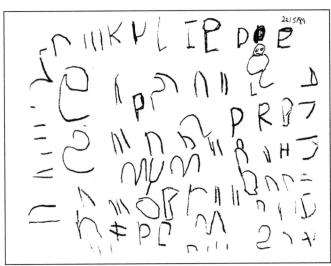

Kylie: 'I am writing my mum a letter.'

Becky and Kylie are relating written text to spoken messages. They need encouragement to keep experimenting and having-a-go with writing to continue their development.

How can I help my child with writing?

- Read to your child and encourage her or him to join in.
- Talk about books before you read them and encourage your child to guess what might happen in the story. Sometimes point to particular words or leave words for your child to predict.
- Build up a collection of favourite books and read them often.
- Take your child to the library to select own books. Don't worry if she or he chooses books which seem too hard — read to or with him/her.
- Write messages to your child and encourage her or him to write replies. Talk about letters, words, spaces, as you write, e.g. 'Mm... Does that word look right? I'll write it again to see... I'll leave a space here before I write the next word.'
- Use a family message board and encourage children to write their own messages.
- Sometimes try written conversations with your child. The idea is to provide a good model without criticising a child's attempts and to encourage him or her to continue writing, e.g.

  Parent writes: *What did you do today?*
  Child replies: *I plad in the avecha plagron*
  Parent writes: *What did you play in the adventure playground?*
  Child replies: *I plad munkees*
  Parent writes: *What did the monkeys' play?*

- Support your child's spelling attempts and praise his or her willingness to have-a-go.
- Provide a special place for your child to write. Equipment such as a small table or desk and a notice board for displaying writing materials such as scrap paper (lined, coloured or plain), used greeting cards, textas, pencils, pens, envelopes and little note-books would provide an excellent environment for children to experiment with writing.
- Encourage your child to make greeting cards for special occasions.
- Talk about the purposes for which you use writing and the advantages of using writing, e.g. telephone messages, recipes or shopping lists to aid memory.
- Use scrap books or books made from spare paper to make personalised books with your child. Glue a photograph or picture chosen by your child into the book and ask your child to tell something about the picture. Let her or him see you write the words and sentences and use for reading. Add more pages and encourage your child to read 'his or her' book.

- Make an alphabet book with your child. As she or he expresses an interest in particular words help her or him to enter words on the appropriate page and keep for use as a personal word bank.
- Draw your child's attention to a variety of print forms such as telephone books, T.V. guides, magazines, street directories and bank stationery.
- Play games making words from plastic or magnetic letters. Discuss similarities and differences in the way words sound or look. Answer your child's questions about print.
- Play games using letter names and sounds, e.g. 'I spy with my little eye'.

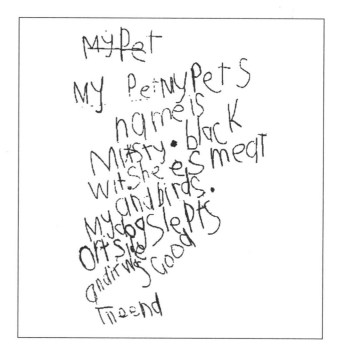

My pet
My pet's name is
Misty. black white.
She eats meat and birds
My dog sleeps outside and
it was good. The end.

Olivia read this to the teacher and looked puzzled when she came to the word 'black'. She said 'I wrote "she is" in my head. I didn't really leave it out.' Olivia knows a lot about writing.

She is displaying all the important behaviours from the Experimental Phase and some behaviours from Early Writing.

Experimental writers have a lot to think about. Praise their efforts.

How can I help my child with writing?

- Praise your child's writing efforts and respond to the message rather than the grammar or spelling. Prominently display your child's writing and demonstrate that you enjoy and value it.
- Have fun writing messages to each other. Try writing reminders, riddles and secret messages.
- Look for opportunities for purposeful writing activities at home. Adults and children can write notes, telephone messages, holiday plans, helper's rosters, greeting cards, letters to friends or to relevant places for information.
- Start a family diary to record special days, funny sayings, weekend activities and other significant events. Include photos, letters cards or other mementos relevant to family. Share reading of the journal with family members.
- Talk with children to help them clarify their thinking about their writing.
- Talk with your child about the sort of writing they are doing at school. If you are involved in writing for work show your child how you write and explain why you are writing.
- Encourage your child to use a word processor or typewriter if one is available.

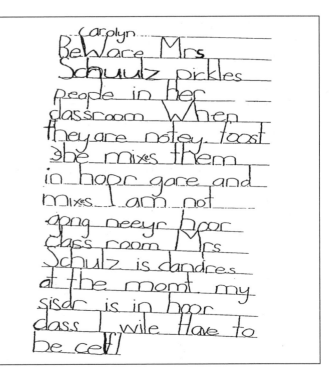

Beware
Beware Mrs Shulz pickles people in her classroom.
When they are naughty first she mixes them in her jar and mixes. I am not going near her classroom. Mrs Shulz is dangerous at the moment my sister is in her class I will have to be careful.

- Read your child's draft writing and comment on the things you like about it. Encourage your child to figure out his or her own answers e.g. have-a-go at spelling a new word and then use a dictionary to check. Provide help if your child asks for it but leave final decisions about writing to the writer.
- If your children ask you to help them 'fix' their writing for publication or for a project, check with the teacher to see if children are using an editing checklist at school and obtain a copy. Work cooperatively with children using the list.
  The following list may be helpful. Read the writing aloud.
  – Can I understand this writing? (Mark any places where the meaning isn't clear)
  – Could the ideas be placed in a better order?
  – Are there any details that could be left out?
  – Does the writing achieve the purpose for which it was written?
  – Have I checked that the punctuation helps to make the meaning clearer?
  – Have I checked the spelling? (Underline any words that cause concern)

Our Father which art in heaven
Hallowed by thy name
Thy Kingdom come
The power and the glory
For Ever and Ever
Amen

- Read to your child every day. Vary the type of material you read. Include interesting newspaper articles, factual books as well as stories, poems and rhymes. Make reading to your child a special quiet time when you can enjoy the experience.
- Give presents that encourage reading and writing. These could include a range of books to read, notebooks, diaries, envelopes, attractive writing paper, pens, coloured felt pens and so on.
- Make sure your child has access to a dictionary that he or she can use. There are simple picture dictionaries and 'Junior' dictionaries available.
- Involve your child in purposeful reading activities such as reading recipes or directions. Assist your child with unfamiliar words but give your child time to have-a-go and praise his or her efforts. Involve children in collecting and writing favourite recipes for the family recipe book.

- Play word games from magazines and newspapers and commercial games such as 'Scrabble', 'Boggle' and so on.
- Try simple crossword puzzles and 'Find the Word' puzzles.
- If your child has access to a computer, have a program which involves her or him in writing or spelling for real purposes, rather than one which simply drills spelling out of context, e.g. solving puzzles, making or completing crosswords, choose your own adventure games.

My Kristy News Plan

When	Who	What	Where	Why	Feelings
Saturday	family cousin I	twisted ankle cut toe	Whitemans Park	Dad play great cricket	alful ~~alful~~

8.5.90 . Last Saturday my family, cousin and I went to W. White mans park to play cricket. When I was walking across the brige . bridge I sliped and twisted my ankle and cut my toe . toe. Then my dad said come and sit down and watch cricket and Then we went home and I felt alful

Early writers need time to talk about their ideas and may need help to make plans.

How can I help my child with writing?

- Praise your child's writing efforts and respond to the message. Show that you enjoy and value your child's writing.
- Ensure that your child has access to a modern dictionary that he or she can use.
- If your child has access to a computer, look out for programs which involve reading, writing or spelling for real purposes, rather than those which simply drill spelling out of context, e.g. solving puzzles, making or completing crosswords, choose your own adventure games.
- When children read independently encourage them to talk about what they are reading. If possible read the books so that you have information to talk about. Ask open questions that allow children to discuss, rather than feel as if they are being interrogated, e.g. What was the book about? Which part was the best?
- Read aloud to your child. Ask the librarian or teacher for suggested titles. Novels by contemporary authors can provide great serials.
- Encourage your child to read newpapers and discuss interesting articles.
- Help your child to write letters requesting information or material for school projects.
- Encourage your child to write to community newspapers about topics of local interest or to a larger paper on more general topics about which they feel strongly.
- Develop consumer awareness by encouraging your child to write to a manufacturer whose product or packaging is unsatisfactory.

Projects: How can parents help?
Many teachers work with children to set guidelines and project plans for children to follow, so talk with your child to see what these entail. If you are unable to ascertain what is expected you may need to seek help from the class teacher.
The following strategies are similar to those used in schools and may provide some guidance so that the children actually do the project (not you!).
- Brainstorm and organise
  This strategy helps your child to see how to order information. Brainstorm all ideas related to the topic. Write each idea on a small piece of paper or card. Write everything that is suggested.
  Move the papers to group ideas that seem related to each other. Draw arrows between words from other categories if they seem relevant. Decide on a sub-heading for each group. Glue the papers when you are satisfied with groupings. This will provide a plan for the project.

- Make decisions
  Draw two columns on a page. In the first column write *What I know* and list all that they know about the topic. In the second column, *What I want to know*, list questions that your child wants answered. Decide where information might come from and jot down resources that could be used.
- Gather information
  Encourage your child to read for information to answer questions and jot down key words as he or she reads. The child then turns the book over and writes information using key words as a guide. (This helps reduce the likelihood of children copying slabs of text.) Gather other supporting material that may be useful e.g. pictures, maps, diagrams etc.
- Set material out under heading and sub-headings and arrange other material. Write information in full for each sub-heading and then do introduction and conclusion. Other inclusions may be contents page, index, glossary of terms and a bibliography.
- Your child may need help to choose and organise appropriate material for projects. This does not mean that parents have to do the whole project. It may be advisable to talk with the your child and the class teacher to make sure.

Children don't always write stories. They write to learn, inform, persuade, compare and express feelings. They write for different purposes and audiences.

How can I help my child with writing?

- Provide a quiet study area for your child.
- Be prepared to discuss writing tasks with your child.
- Encourage your child to continue to read and write for information and pleasure.
- Take your child to see suitable 'live' theatre performances.
- Discuss current events.
- Talk about the mass media and their influence on society.
- Encourage your child to use writing to get things done e.g. letters to politicians, newspapers etc.
- Encourage your child to use writing to express feelings. Respect his or her privacy if he or she chooses to keep personal diaries or letters.
- Play word games, talk about word meanings.
- Encourage your child to use dictionaries and thesauruses independently.
- Understand that the process of writing and refining writing for publication takes time.
- Understand that writing is for different purposes and audiences.
- Understand that different types of writing require different language, setting out and special vocabulary e.g. a business letter is not the same as a letter to a pen pal.

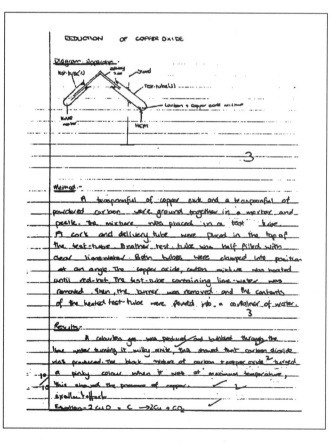

When the purpose of writing changes, so does the form.

Spelling

Very few people can spell every single word correctly. Most of us, even if we are good spellers, make some mistakes from time to time. The important thing is that we know how to attack a word which is difficult or unfamiliar. Good spellers are people who know what to do when they are stuck.

If we are asked what we do when we attempt to spell a word, most of us would say 'Sound it out'. However, when we stop to think about it we realise that sounding out is only one of the things we do. There are lots of words we need to spell that we cannot sound out.

Here are a few of the strategies good spellers use:
- they have a store of words they can spell automatically — beginning spellers know words like *am, here, the, come, were, was,* etc.
- they sound words out — beginning spellers can sound out words like *cat, Mum, Dad, sit, fat,* etc.
- they know many common letter patterns, so they know when a word looks right — beginning spellers know patterns like *sh, th, ch, ing;* later on, *ought, ious,* etc.
- they can divide words into syllables — beginning spellers can do this with words like *dingo, seven, garden*
- they can make links between the meaning of words and their spelling — beginning spellers don't do this much. Later on connections would be made between words like *sign, signature, signal* or *circle, circumference, circumvent*
- they work out spelling rules for themselves
- they use people and dictionaries to help them — beginning spellers can ask a friend even if they can't yet use a dictionary

It is very important that children are encouraged to have a go at spelling words they don't know when they are writing. If they do not have a go they will not get the chance to practise these important strategies. If children only use words which they know they can spell, they may never make a mistake, but they will not get the chance to become good adult spellers. Praise your child for having a go!

In the following pages you will find the Developmental Continuum for Spelling which you can use to follow your child's literacy development. There are also some suggestions for helping your child at each phase of development. You will already be doing many of these things, but you might find one or two new ideas that would be fun to try.

Spelling

Phases

Phase 1: Preliminary Spelling

In this phase children become aware that print carries a message. They experiment with scribble that looks like writing as they try to mimic written language. Their 'writing' is not readable by others. They have not yet made the links between the sounds of spoken words and the letters of written words.

Phase 2: Semi-Phonetic Spelling

In this phase children start to make the links between the sounds of spoken words and the letters of written words. They may write a whole word using one, two or three letters. Sometimes children write words in their own unconventional way; sometimes they may copy letters.

Phase 3: Phonetic Spelling

In this phase children are able to provide an almost perfect match between letters and sounds. Letters are chosen on the basis of sound, often without regard for conventional spelling. Children often consistently use their own home-made rules resulting in spelling that may not look conventional.

The writer:

- shows understanding that print carries a message by saying things like *This says 'We did some cooking for our afternoon tea'*
- uses marks that look like letters or numbers to represent writing
- uses some real letters and numbers — these may be mixed up with pretend writing
- recognises own name or part of it in print e.g. Steven points to a STOP sign and says *That's like my name*
- writes some letters of own name correctly
- uses some known letters repeatedly, often using letters from own name
- reacts to print in the environment e.g. logos, television advertisements, street signs, fast food signs
- begins to 'write' from left to right and top to bottom on a page
- knows some letter names e.g. A = *ay*, B = *Bee*, C = *See*
- sings alphabet songs
- is willing to have a go at representing speech in print form — this may look like scribble
- asks questions about printed words and messages
- likes to talk about own 'writing'
- knows that writing and drawing are different e.g. *Mummy reads the black bits*

Turn to page 40 for ideas that will support your child at this phase.

The writer:

- relies on the sounds of a word that are most obvious to him or her. These may be the first, last or middle sounds e.g. D (down), DN (down), DON (down), KT (kitten), WT (went), BAB (baby), LRFT (elephant)
- uses the first letter of each word in a sentence e.g. W D I W T R S. J N W N S Z (One day I went to the Royal Show. Johnny went on the Sizzler.)
- uses letter names to represent sounds, syllables or words e.g. AT (eighty), CD (seed)
- writes one or two letters for sounds and may add random letters to complete the word e.g. *greim* (grass)
- begins to use some common letter patterns e.g. *th* (the) and *Bck* (bike)
- uses a small number of sight words correctly e.g. *I, me, mum, the, my*
- is aware that some words rhyme
- leaves spaces between 'words' e.g. *I bn sik* (I've been sick)
- is willing to have a go at writing
- recognises and copies some words
- confidently experiments with writing e.g. fills out bank forms mimicking an adult
- asks questions and talks about writing, words and letters
- copies words or letters from the environment e.g. writes Milk copied from milk carton

Turn to page 41 for ideas that will support your child at this phase.

The writer:

- chooses letters on the basis of sound e.g. kaj (cage), tabl (table), birgla (burglar), vampia (vampire), spidr (spider), chucd (chucked)
- makes and uses own rules e.g. livd (lived), Chucd (chucked), becoz (because), woz (was), dor (door), sor (saw), wor (wore)
- represents the sounds of letters logically, but not necessarily accurately e.g. oshan (ocean), nacher (nature), consert (concert), thort (thought)
- adds extra vowels e.g. miu (my), beofore (before), crecuea (creature), derum (drum)
- represents past tense according to the sounds heard e.g. stopt (stopped), watcht (watched), livd (lived)
- uses the letter 'r' to represent the final syllable of a word e.g. watr (water), mothr (mother)
- confuses short vowel sounds e.g. locing (lurking), pell (pill), yallow (yellow), pan (pen), lat (let)
- when two consonants occur together, may omit one of them e.g. fog (frog), mik (milk), plak (plank)
- uses some letter names in spelling e.g. awa (away), gav (gave), xellent (excellent), lrst (last)
- uses some known words to spell other words e.g. mathursday (mother's day), apresheeight (appreciate)
- represents each syllable with some letters e.g. telefon (telephone), vampia (vampire), apon (upon), mome (mummy)
- is keen to have a go at spelling words in different ways
- feels confident as a writer and responds to praise
- is able to spell words from favourite book on interest e.g. telescope, dinosaur

Turn to page 42 for ideas that will support your child at this phase.

Phase 4: Transitional Spelling (from sounds to structures)

In this phase children realise that sounding out a word does not always work, so they need to take more notice of how words look and the common patterns of letters which are found in English spelling. Children are beginning to proof read their work and use an increasing number of words they can spell correctly. Children may remain in this phase for some time.

Phase 5: Independent Spelling

In this phase writers have become aware of the many patterns and rules that are characteristic of the English spelling system. They use a range of methods of attacking a new word, for example sounding out, seeing if the word looks right, looking a word up in a dictionary, using a common letter pattern, thinking of the meaning of the word. They are able to recognise when a word does not look right, and know a great many words which they can spell automatically.

... The Princy Adventure. Once upon a time thier lived a hansom prince his mother was dying and he had to find some fruit to qurer her. In the kingdom there were no fruit trees ...

Originally or in the start the snale had skin like a frog not like the scales it has today. This is a story of how the snake got scales.
On day Sugalfe the snake was slithering round when he heard his friends talking to eachother He decided to join them and so he slithered over. They were discussing a problem they had. The chief snake was dying and he had sent out messages to anyone who could convince him that they were good enough for his place. Anyone who decided they were good enough had to dress in a particular way that shows leaders

The writer

- places vowels in every syllable e.g. hansom (handsome), holaday (holiday), castel (castle), qurar (cure), kingdom
- is beginning to use common patterns of letters such as thousend (thousand), cort (cought), doller (dollar)
- uses a silent 'e' as an alternative for spelling long vowel sounds e.g. mite (might), biye (buy), moste (most), rane (rain)
- correctly inserts a vowel before the consonant at the end of a word e.g. *brother* instead of *brothr*; *water* instead of *watr*
- spells word endings such as ..tion, ...ious, ...ight, ...ough conventionally
- includes all the correct letters, but may sequence them incorrectly e.g. siad (said), yuo (you), shose (shoes), thier (their)
- is beginning to use double letters correctly e.g. stopped, apple, necessary
- is able to recognise when a common word is spelt incorrectly
- is beginning to use the meaning of a word to help with the spelling e.g. sign, signature, signal
- is extending the number of words they can spell automatically
- is beginning to use knowledge of parts of words to aid spelling, e.g. re/vise, un/healthy, clean/li/ness, tight/ly, wonder/ful,
- uses resources such as dictionaries, thesauruses and topic lists to check own spelling
- has an interest in playing with words and enjoys using them
- is willing to have a go at spelling specialised words, such as words used in science and social studies e.g. experament (experiment), electrisity (electricity)

Turn to page 43 for ideas that will support your child at this phase.

The writer:

- knows many patterns and rules that characterise the English spelling system
- makes generalisations so that they can apply their knowledge in different situations e.g. rules for adding suffixes, selection of appropriate letter patterns
- uses spelling references such as dictionaries, thesauruses and resource books appropriately
- can spell a large range of words automatically, including complicated and sophisticated words
- uses context to distinguish between homonyms such as **wind** the clock and a strong **wind** and homophones such as there, their, they're and to, two, too
- accurately spells words with uncommon spelling patterns and words with irregular spelling e.g. rhythm, aisle, quay, choir
- successfully proof reads own writing
- realises that society expects people to spell correctly
- recognises word origins and uses this information to make meaningful associations between words e.g. automatic, automotive, autonomous

Turn to page 44 for ideas that will support your child at this phase.

How can I help my child with spelling?

- Read favourite books again and again. Encourage children to join in and help turn the pages at the right time. Talk a lot about the pictures, but make it quite clear that the story, which stays the same every time, is read from the print and not the pictures.
- When you are reading stories, sometimes comment on interesting or unusual words, pointing and saying, for instance, 'What a long word!'
- Look at alphabet books with your child. Using letter names, talk about the letters and the sounds they make in relation to the pictures. Make connections with family names or objects in the room.
- Sing alphabet songs together. If you don't know any, make one up by singing the alphabet to a well-known tune.
- Say nursery rhymes with your child and let him/her contribute the last word or phrase.
- Talk about print in the shops, street and on television. For instance, 'That says 'STOP' or 'No dogs' or 'EXIT''. Talk about print in advertisements or shop signs.
- Draw attention to your child's written name as often as you can. For instance, write the name in the front of books, help her/him write her/his name in birthday cards, label paintings etc.
- Draw attention to the initial sound of your child's name. Connect this with the initial letter.
- Encourage your child to recognise the first letter of his/her name when it appears as the first letter in other contexts, for instance, Sam might say, pointing to the S in STOP, 'That's my name' and you might reply 'Yes, that's S for Sam'.
- Put labels on things, for instance, 'Annabel's toy box'.
- Provide scrap paper and crayons or pencils. Encourage your child to draw and scribble. Show pleasure when she/he starts to make letter-like formations. When real letters start appearing, don't worry if they are mixed up with numerals, scribble or simulated letters. Display all their efforts and show them to friends. Value all early attempts to write, whatever form they take.
- Write notes, shopping lists, cards etc. in front of your child, explaining what you are writing.
- Play games in the car, recognising the letters and numbers on the numberplates.
- When you go to the bank or post office, let your child 'fill in a form' while she/he waits for you.

Value your child's early attempts to write.

I'm playing outside

Clifford went to the park.

part of name

Chloe   21-10-92   Preliminary - Pre P.

repeats some known alphabet symbols / often uses letters from own name

uses writing like symbols to represent written language

The farmer is out at the museum and he will come home soon because the cows are waiting.

assigns a message to own symbols.

How can I help my child with spelling?

- Sometimes point to words as you read to your child, but do not interrupt the flow of the story unless the child asks a question. Comment on long words, short words, interesting words. Comment on the special features of these words. When you talk about a word, *circle* it with your finger. If you *point* at a word the child might confuse the word with the letter your finger is pointing at.
- Borrow a set of magnetic letters from the toy library and encourage your child to play with them, making her/his name or any other words.
- Continue to share your writing with your child on every possible occasion: when noting telephone messages, making shopping lists, filling in forms, writing letters or cards etc.
- Encourage your child to write on every possible occasion. Give him/her paper when you are writing so that she/he can write beside you. Write for real reasons such as greeting cards, letters, lists, messages etc. Always accept and value the writing and use it for the intended purpose.
- Always encourage your child to have-a-go at spelling; only give concrete help when it is demanded.
- Show amazement and delight when your child uses the initial letters or clusters of two or three letters when writing words. Do not correct the child, but value the approximation. If possible model the correct spelling in context. For instance, if the child writes on a picture 'I M rl My BCK' you can write 'I like to see you riding your bike'.
- If your child is trying to learn a word, help by:
  - encouraging him/her to have-a-go at spelling it first, to see how much of the word he/she already knows;
  - point out that she/he knows a lot about the word already, so she/he will only have to learn (2) letters;
  - use the 'look - cover - write - check' routine, stressing that the 'look' is for focusing on the unknown letters. For instance, if the child has spelled 'went' as 'we', the only bit that has to be learned is 'we*nt*'.
- Play *I spy with my little eye…*
- Continue to play numberplate games in the car, thinking of words which start with the letters.
- Continue to make attractive paper, note pads and pencils available to your child. If possible create a little writing table for his/her own use.
- Help your child to use a simple picture dictionary.

Praise all attempts to read and write. Talk about the message of the print.

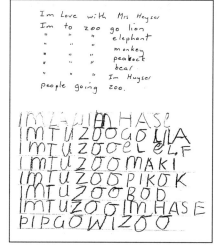

I'm love with Mrs Heyser
I'm to zoo go lion
I'm to zoo go elephant
I'm to zoo go monkey
I'm to zoo go peacock
I'm to zoo go bear
I'm to zoo I'm Heyser
People going zoo

I W TO SACAS

I went to see a crane at school.

early Year 1

Dylan
iWenttsFil.

I went to see a film.

How can I help my child with spelling?

- Continue to read to your child each day. Discuss interesting or funny words or words with unusual spellings.
- Make up mnemonics together to help with the spelling of difficult words, for instance, NIGHT—I'm Going Home Tonight, or, if having problems with a specific word ending such as 'ious'—I Owe U (you) Something
- Play increasingly sophisticated numberplate games in the car, for instance, trying to make a word which incorporates all the letters, or a nonsense phrase from the initial letters, such as HHC—Happy Hippos Croak.
- When your child writes or brings work home it is very important that you focus on what has been written, not on the spelling. If you do mention spelling, always focus on the words which have been spelled right, rather than on the mistakes. Talk about mistakes in terms of 'You had a jolly good try at spelling that word, didn't you?'. Always encourage risk-taking and having-a-go and show that you value all attempts.
- Encourage your child to try simple crossword puzzles and acrostics.
- Play simple word games such as 'Hang the Man'. If it is possible encourage relatives to give commercial word games for birthdays.
- Enjoy jokes and riddles with your child, especially those which play on words.
- Try and set up a desk or writing table in a well lit area. Have available a children's dictionary and thesaurus. Keep a good supply of note pads, scrap paper and attractive writing paper as well as an ample supply of pens and pencils.
- Encourage your child to make birthday cards, write thank-you letters, send post cards and the like.
- Help your child use the 'look, cover, write, check' method for learning words, concentrating on the part of the word he/she is not sure of rather than the whole word. Help the child divide the word into syllables.
- Encourage children to read through their work and underline any words they are not sure about. Don't do this for them, and don't draw attention to those they might have missed. Encourage them to think about the words they have identified and try alternative spellings, choosing the one which looks right. When you assist, help cooperatively rather than *telling* as an expert.

Encourage your child to try different ways to spell a word.

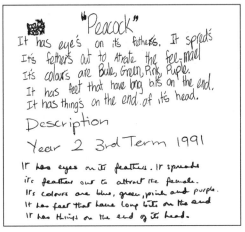

My Mum is overdue.

Peacock
It has eyes on its feathers. It spreads
its feathers out to attract the female.
Its colours are blue, green, pink and purple.
It has feet that have long bits on the end.
It has things on the end of its head.

On my birthday we had an ice-cream cake and for tea we had a pizza. Mum made the pizza and when we finished we got to have some chips and after everyone finished we had the ice-cream cake.

How can I help my child with spelling?

- Continue to read to your child regularly, discussing the way the author has used words and any interesting features of words that you notice.
- Do crossword puzzles together and play word games whenever you can.
- Ensure that your child reads a wide range of books, magazines, TV guides, recipes and instructions for making or operating things. Make good use of the library to extend the range of stories and informational books your child can read.
- Continue to keep a writing area well supplied with attractive paper and pens. Encourage your child to make birthday and Christmas cards and write letters, cards etc.
- Encourage your child to keep a journal. This may be specially useful when on holiday or travelling. Respect her/his privacy.
- Always be interested in work your child brings home and ensure that you focus on what is being said rather than on spelling. If spelling is mentioned praise him/her for having-a-go and making a good approximation, rather than commenting on errors.
- When children are trying to learn a word:
  - first let them have-a-go at spelling it.
  - then note all the letters which are correct.
  - if some are incorrect, it will probably be for a good reason, for instance, a child might spell 'handsome' *hansom*. If this happens, praise the child for having a sensible go and spelling the word as she/he thinks it sounds.
  - then divide the word into the syllables *hand* and *some*, both of which the child will be able to spell. This will bring much better results than simply gazing at the word in an attempt to learn it.
  - if, on the other hand, the child has reversed letters, for instance *peice* instead of *piece,* help the child to focus only on the letters that are reversed rather than the whole word. 'Piece has ie in the middle, like pie'.
  - now employ the 'look, cover, write, check' method.
- If your child is having problems with spelling, two things may help:
  - providing encouragement by counting the words that are *right*, instead of the words that are wrong.
  - Learning one or two words well, rather than failing to learn ten or twenty. Talk this through with the teacher, who will know what is best for your child.

Talk to children about different words and meanings.

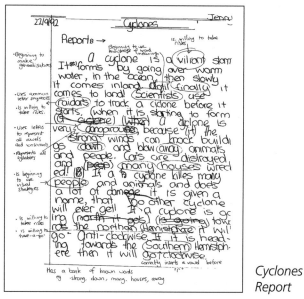

INVADERS SPACE ALIENS

Mars 4000 A.D. Saturday
Space aliens have attacked people living on the moon. The people living on the moon said 'We must destroy the space aliens before they destroy our planet.' At the moment the main colony is full of frightened people. The earth has sent someone to help the people living on the moon to help fight the space aliens.

Cyclones Report

A cyclone is a violent storm. It forms by going over warm water in the ocean, then slowly it comes inland until finally it comes to land! Scientists use radar to track a cyclone before it starts.
A cyclone is very dangerous, because the strong winds can knock buildings down and blow away animals and people. Cars are destroyed and many houses wrecked. If a cyclone kills many people and animals and does a lot of damage it is given a name that no other cyclone will ever get. If a cyclone is going towards the northern hemisphere it will go anti-clockwise. If it is heading towards the southern hemisphere, then it will go clockwise.

How can we enjoy exploring words together?

- Go to the library together and talk about the books you are choosing.
- Discuss newspaper articles, thinking about words which have been coined from other sources, jargon words which are coming into vogue and words which have been invented to suit a particular context. Be critical of word choice and use.
- Read and discuss articles in periodicals and newspapers which focus on word derivations and the evolution of meaning. Some of these appear regularly and can become a regular feature of family life.
- See who can complete a crossword, acrostic or quiz first. Discuss clues and share insights.
- Play family word games. Many on the market are equally attractive for grandparents, parents and older children.
- Discuss words you are not sure of yourself and ask for help in remembering them (how many M's in immeasurable?).

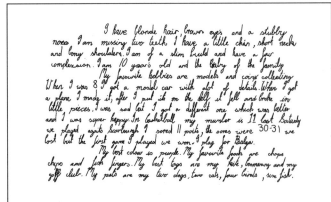

Encourage children to proof read their writing.